THE TITHE:
Blessing or Curse?

by

Dr. Michael Arkman Bonilla

Bonilla Archaeological Research™
www.arkman.net
www.akjv.org

Foreword by
Anonymous

Llumina
Christian
Books

ISBN: 978-1-62550-476-0

About the Author

Biblical Archaeologist and Author, Dr. Michael Arkman Bonilla, has been called, chosen and anointed by God to share, witness and minister the gospel of Jesus through archaeology. His calling, as instructed by the Lord is first to the church and then to the rest of the world. Michael's field and research work span 7 trips to the Middle East which include (1) tour to Petra, Jordan; (2) tours to Eastern Turkey and (6) tours to Israel. His work in Petra, Jordan was to document and research the remains of Petra and tied them in with the book of Obadiah. He has worked on the remains of Noah's Ark, and the first archaeologist to obtain and record the latitude, longitude and elevation of the remains of Noah's Ark on October 11th of 2000, using his Garmin GPS handheld device. He has recovered several specimens of petrified wood, coprolite (fossilized animal dropping) and other artifacts. His work in Israel has included identifying the "borrowed" Tomb Of Jesus (located in the Garden Tomb, Jerusalem); Further documenting the Cross Site of Jesus also located in the Garden Tomb; Researched the area of the ashen remains of the City of Gomorrah (one of the 5 Cities of the Plain), was able to obtain specimens of ash and over 125 specimens of Brimstone (sulphur) as mentioned in Genesis 19:24.

Dr. Bonilla is a biblical archaeologist who obtained his Ph.D. in May of 2002, with high honors (GPA of 3.93) in Archaeology from Parkwood University, (originally based out in London), through an accelerated distance learning program. His (24+ page) doctoral dissertation & titled "Discovery of Noah's Ark" which covers the aspects of scientific investigations and testings along with scriptural references from the Bible. He earned his Bachelor's of Science/Masters of Science degrees in Criminal Justice with a (GPA of 3.8), from Columbia University. Michael clearly states that it was the Holy Spirit's anointing and gifting that has made a way for his knowledge, understanding and prophetic insight. Having degrees is great but without the Holy Spirit illuminating and guiding my path, I would be totally lost.

On July of 2004, he released and published his first poetic work titled: "DISCOVERING BIBLICAL TRUTH, UNCOVERING GOD'S FAITH". Being fluent in both English & Spanish, Michael has been seen on TV and heard on radio, but his first love is sharing the gospel through archaeology in a church setting, his second preference would be sharing the gospel of Jesus in any bible college or university. His main World Class PowerPoint presentation is titled "The 5 Major Discoveries" which covers the following discoveries: Remains of Noah's Ark; The Exodus Route including Mount Sinai in Saudi Arabia; Sodom and Gomorrah; The Cross Site of Jesus and the Ark of the Covenant with the blood of Jesus on the Mercy-Seat. His other major presentation is titled: Creation Evolution and Noah's Ark.

Intelligent Design is one of his favorite subjects, although the discovery of the Ark of the Covenant and the blood of Jesus is the number one passion of his heart! Most of his presentations have also been translated in Spanish, and are ready to be presented with the purpose of impacting the Latino community.

On March 20th of 2010, Michael pioneered the "Conferencia de Arqueología" and presented "The 5 Major Discoveries". It was the first conference of its kind and the first ever presented in the world in Spanish. On Father's Day, June 20th of 2010, Michael was honored and affirmed as an "Archaeological Pastor" by a prophetic word received from the Lord via the late prophet Pedro Martinez Jr.

On March 21st of 2012, (via prophetic word), Michael was commissioned to revise God's only preserved word in the King James Bible. This ministry project began on June 5th, 2013 and was completed by September 12th, 2013. The new title of God's only preserved word is Arkman's King James Holy Bible, it can be downloaded through www.akjv.org.

On December 25th of 2013, Christmas night at 11:57pm, the Lord spoke to Michael a clear prophetic word:"Tithing impoverishes My people and it's the driving force that enriches church leaders". Right there, Michael understood that the Lord wanted him to put together a PowerPoint presentation on the tithe! Michael at first hesitated because this is not a very popular subject amongst church leaders if you are called to deliver clarity, understanding and correction to them all in regards of the most controversial subject in the church today.

That said, on May 4th of 2014, Michael was strongly impressed of the Holy Spirit to begin writing a book on the tithe. This was clearly not his idea but when God instructed him to put this thing together, and gave him all the information personally, then God confirms all the information with His word (in this case, Arkman's King James Bible), and seals this presentation with an unprecedented (5) prophetic words to be incorporated into "His" PowerPoint presentation... Michael realized then, that the Holy Spirit had given him, the most anointed, accurate and complete teaching on "The Tithe" in the world!!!

Michael delivers with his own unique style, a combination of biblical knowledge with a prophetic insight. Prepare yourself for an awesome and inspirational time of spiritual revelation and knowledge! All the presentations and or seminars can be customized according to your organization, or church needs. You can contact him by telephone or e-mail by visiting www.arkman.net or www.akjv.org

Dedication

I dedicate this book, to every New Testament believer that has suffered financially and has been victimized because of the ignorance, arrogance and lack of understanding of God's Word by our church leaders in the area of giving and finances. I pray that you would always find within the corridors of your heart, the gift of forgiveness.

Acknowledgment

I need to acknowledge my spiritual father for helping me proof-read this book and for always provoking me to a greater and deeper relationship with Jesus and His Holy Word! He taught me many years ago that when discussing doctrinal differences and or issues... personal thoughts and opinions must always take second place to God's authoritative word known as the Bible.

Table of Contents

Foreword

I have been a pastor on Long Island, New York for over ten years, and was taught many years ago by our pastors, that the tithe belongs to God and it is holy unto the Lord. The scripture referenced was always from Malachi, chapter 3 and verses 8 to 11. I was one of those pastors that imposed the tithe on my congregation!

My associate pastor sent me a link and urged me to watch Mike's video on YouTube™ called "The Tithe: Man Has Robbed God". Wow, that really opened my eyes. I watched this video at least 4 times with my husband. We felt the peace of the Holy Spirit, and then as we prayed together like we always do, we also did repent and asked God for forgiveness. The very next day, I called for an emergency meeting with my leaders. I first addressed all my associate pastors and deacons. I made them watch the video, then some did try to justify their beliefs, but ultimately everyone yielded to the authority of the Holy Scriptures.

In the last few weeks, ever since we all discussed the video and how to share this "new-found" revelation/knowledge with the congregation, about the blessed truth on the tithe; we've all noticed an increase of the power, grace and love of God throughout our two services we hold every week. I also noticed my people seem to be so much happier!

I thank and praise God for revelation knowledge and understanding. Hallelujah, and praise the living God for His mercy and grace! I also want to thank God for my brother in Christ Mike, for his obedience and sensitivity to the Spirit of God and for graciously accepting my request in not mentioning my personal name or my church's name in his book.

In Christ's unconditional love,
Anonymous

Introduction

I have always said that knowledge and understanding at times, seem to complement each other and on other occasions, seem to clash with each other! The reason I state this fact, is because most church leaders have a lot of knowledge on the Old Testament ordinance known as "The Tithe", yet most lack its true definition, meaning and understanding. This can easily be observed in most of the Christian churches throughout this side of the world including Christians in the "Latino community".

It is very clear scripturally, from both the Old and New Testament scriptures... that the tithe was to be only implemented and or imposed strictly to the children of Israel and all the priests living under the Old Covenant Law, until the time after Jesus' death, burial and resurrection. The Old Covenant was canceled by the introduction of the New Covenant.

Have you ever wondered, why the gospels record our Lord and Savior Jesus, paying taxes to Caesar, but no records exist in the New Testament of Jesus paying or giving tithes? Did you know that Paul and every disciple of Jesus did not pay tithes either? Do you still wonder why Jesus, Paul and or anyone else in the New Testament did not teach any Jews or Gentiles to tithe either? Were you aware that in the New Testament there are no records either of Jesus, Paul and the rest of the apostles collecting or receiving tithes?

This book contains the most accurate and complete teaching on "The Tithe" in the world! It navigates from Genesis to Hebrews, while delivering understanding, clarity to the New Testament believer while bringing correction to church leaders. When God commissioned me to write this book, I had no notes on the subject but all the information was handed to me by the Holy Spirit. God confirmed all the information He gave me with His "Word" and divinely sealed His work with an unprecedented (5) prophetic words, that He clearly spoke to me (and also are listed towards the end of this book) to specifically warn, rebuke and correct all church leaders that impose the tithe on God's people!

Let every man or woman be declared a liar, but the Word of God will always stand and remain true! There comes a time that we need to discard or disregard man's opinion and traditions and replace them with sound biblical doctrine! Understanding the scriptures comes from the Holy Spirit, as stated in (Luke 24:45 AKJV) and not from a New York Times Best Seller book.

God wants to set His church free from the curse and bondage of the tithe by delivering clarity, understanding and correction to church leaders today! Now, will you still stand in God's way or will you yield to the Holy Spirit?

THE TITHE:

Blessing or Curse?

This is what the Holy Spirit is saying now!

"He that has an ear, let him hear what the Spirit says unto the churches."

Rev 2:7 AKJV

The New Testament tithe: Has been birthed out of the doctrine of the commandments of men.

"But in vain they do worship Me, teaching for doctrines the commandments of men."

Matt 15:9 AKJV

This is not a bible study!

This is a prophetic message to all church leaders!

Have you ever wondered...

What teachings and doctrines have been handed down to our church leaders for hundreds of years that "may" or "may not" line up with the word of God, that's been personally designed for the New Testament born again believer? For example... tithe, sabbath, rapture, etc.

This prophetic message...

Exposes one of Satan's highest levels of deception: Imposing the tithe on God's people! The Bible says...

"...there is no truth in him... for he is a liar, and the father of it."

John 8:44 AKJV

"... for Satan himself is transformed into an angel of light."

2 Cor 11:14 AKJV

Instructed by Timothy...

"Study to show thyself approved unto God, a workman that needs not to be ashamed, rightly dividing the word of truth."

2 Tim 2:15 AKJV

Authorized by Timothy...

"All Scripture is given by inspiration of God, and profitable for doctrine, for reproof, for correction, for instruction in righteousness: That the man of God may be perfect..."

2 Tim 3:16,17 AKJV

Definitions...

<u>Old Covenant</u>: *refers to the covenant between God and the children of Israel based on the Mosaic Law. The Old Covenant was in effect up to the time **<u>before</u>** Jesus' death, burial and resurrection.*

<u>New Testament</u>: *in effect after Jesus' death, burial and resurrection which **<u>fulfilled</u>** the Old Law and Covenant requirements. It's associated with the New Testament and the Lordship of Jesus.*

<u>In context</u>: *taking parts of a written statement and or speech that follows a particular passage which contributes to the understanding of its meaning.*

THE TITHE:

Blessing or Curse?

Tithe Facts...

__Tithe__: *a tenth of the produce of the earth consecrated and set apart for special purposes. The dedication of a tenth to God was recognized as a duty before the time of Moses. Abraham paid tithes to Melchizedek (Genesis 14:20 and Hebrews 7:6).*

The first Mosaic Law on this subject is recorded in Leviticus 27:30-32. The paying of the tithes was an important part of the Jewish religious worship. The neglect of this duty was sternly rebuked by the prophets (Amos 4:4 and Malachi 3:8-10). It cannot be affirmed that the Old Testament law of tithes is binding on the Christian Church.

(Referenced from Easton's Bible Dictionary)

Tithe, Tithes and Tithing are mentioned:

1). 40 x's throughout the Bible (32 verses)

2). 32 x's in the Old Testament

3). 8 x's in the New Testament: Jesus (3) & Paul (5) x's

Tithe, Tithes and Tithing are...

1). Not taught in the New Testament

2). Not instructed in the New Testament

3). Not collected in the New Testament

4). Not received in the New Testament

5). Not paid by Jesus, His disciples or Paul in the N. T.

6). Not referred as money, but only as "agricultural produce" in both the Old and New Testaments

The Old Testament

The tithe first mentioned in Genesis...

"And blessed be the most High God, which has delivered thine enemies into thy hand. And he[1] gave him[2] tithes..."

Gen 14:20 AKJV

1 = Abraham   2 = Melchizedek

Questions...

1). Did God tell Abraham to tithe to Melchizedek?

2). What exactly did Abraham tithe?

3). How many times Abraham tithe to Melchizedek?

Answers...

1). Absolutely not!

2). From the spoils of the war!

3). Only once!

"And all the tithe of the land, whether of the seed of the land, or of the fruit of the tree, is the LORD'S: it is holy unto the LORD."

Lev 27:30 AKJV

*** <u>Note:</u>

It is here, in this verse where the tithe becomes law and "holy" unto the LORD and to be observed by Israel!

Studying Malachi in context...

"... the word of the LORD <u>to Israel</u> by Malachi."

Malachi 1:1 AKJV

"And now, <u>O ye priests</u>, this commandment is for you."

Malachi 2:1 AKJV

"... therefore <u>ye sons of Jacob</u> are not consumed..."

Malachi 3:6 AKJV

*** <u>Note</u>:

In (Malachi 1:1 & 2:1), God is speaking to the children of Israel, and then to all the (ye) priests and by the time we get to (Malachi 3:6), God is speaking to all the (ye) sons Of Jacob! God is not speaking nor was He addressing the New Testament born again believer!

"Will a man rob God? yet ye have robbed Me. But ye say, Where have we robbed Thee? In tithes and offerings. Ye are cursed with a curse: for ye have robbed Me, even this whole nation."

Malachi 3:8,9 AKJV

*** <u>Note:</u>

In Malachi 3:8, it is the primary scripture that most church leaders use to impose the tithe on the New Testament believer. The neglect of this duty was sternly rebuked by the prophet Malachi to the children of Israel also including all the priests.

"Bring ye all the tithes into the storehouse, that there may be food in My house, and prove Me now at this moment, says the LORD of Hosts, If I will not open you the windows of heaven, and pour you out a blessing, that there shall not be room enough to receive it."

Malachi 3:10 AKJV

*** _Note:_

In Malachi 3:10, the tithe was clearly food and not monetary. The storehouse it's not a bank or financial institution but rather a place where food and agricultural produce would be stored for an unspecific amount of time for the glorious and sole purpose of feeding the poor! This particular scripture from Malachi, it's the only place where God challenges Israel to prove Him by offering tithes and in return, God would pour out a blessing, that there shall not be room enough to receive it...

But, if the tithe really applied to us today, churches would be flooded with an unprecedented overflow of financial blessings and praise reports pouring in weekly. Meaning that everyone who tithes, would never have need or lack in anything on a weekly basis (divine provision).

This kind of supernatural dimension of blessing never occurs. You might have an isolated case, where God supernaturally blesses the giver beyond measure... but it's rare! I believe Malachi 3:10, to be the "smoking gun" scripture that justifies for the tithe, not to be imposed or enforced on God's people today.

"And I will rebuke the devourer for your sakes, and he shall not destroy the fruits of your ground; neither shall your vine cast her fruit before the time in the field, says the LORD of Hosts."

Malachi 3:11 AKJV

*** Note:

Fruit(s) referring to agricultural produce and not money!!! You will find out through the Bible that when the tithe is mentioned, it is always referred to as agricultural produce and never money!

The New Testament

Is the tithe taught in the New Testament?

"Woe unto you, scribes and Pharisees, hypocrites! for ye pay tithes of <u>mint</u>, <u>dill</u> and <u>cummin</u>, and have neglected the weightier matters of the law, judgment, mercy, and faith: these should ye to have done, and not to leave the other undone."

Matthew 23:23 AKJV

"But woe unto you, Pharisees! For ye tithe <u>mint</u> and <u>medicinal herb</u> and all manner of <u>herbs</u>, and pass over judgment and the love of God: these ought ye to have done, and not to leave the other undone."

Luke 11:42 AKJV

*** _Note:_

In Matthew 23:23 and Luke 11:42... Jesus and every person on earth, were still under the Old Covenant Law, since Jesus had not died, been buried or resurrected yet! Jesus did not have a choice but to commend the Pharisees for tithing. He is the Word, and He will always be true to His Word! Here we clearly see that in both gospels of Matthew and Luke, the substances being tithed are mints, dills, cummin and herbs (agricultural produce) and not money!!!

Fact: The gospels of Matthew, Mark, Luke and John contain a total of 89 chapters. In 84 of those chapters (94½%), we find Jesus and everyone else on earth, were still under the Old Covenant, since Jesus had not resurrected yet; therefore the "better" or the New Covenant had not been established yet!

When and where... did Paul mention the tithe?

"For this Melchizedek, king of Salem... who met Abraham returning from the slaughter of the kings, and blessed him; To whom Also Abraham gave a tenth part of all... Now consider how great this man was unto whom even the patriarch Abraham gave the tenth of the spoils."

Hebrews 7:1,2,4 AKJV

In Hebrews chapter 7, Paul addresses the greatness of Melchizedek and His priesthood (the main point), and then mentions the patriarch Abraham giving a tithe (only once as recorded in Genesis) to Melchizedek! Abraham tithed to Melchizedek "once" and it was of the spoils of the war and not what he owned, possessed or earned.

New Testament search and inquiry on...

1). Why are there no records in the New Testament of the tithe being paid, taught, collected, or received by Jesus, Paul and or any other disciple?

Maybe because the tithe was not paid, taught, collected or received by anyone after Jesus resurrected. That's why no records exist!

2). Why do many church leaders impose the tithe?

Many church leaders do not trust God to financially provide for their church needs and salaries because of lack of faith, deception, ignorance, love of money or worse "knowingly" not living right before God... It's one of these!!!

Monetary system during the time of Jesus

While living on this planet (as a man), the methods of payments to buy goods and services, to pay taxes and temple services including the tithe were mainly the Syrian, Roman and Jewish coins. As a matter of fact, Genesis 24:22, mentions the use of the shekel.

Warnings from Timothy, Titus and Peter...

"Now the Spirit speaks expressly, that in the latter times some shall depart from the faith, paying attention to seducing spirits, and doctrines of devils; Speaking lies in hypocrisy;..."

1 Timothy 4:1-2 AKJV

"For there are many unruly and vain talkers and deceivers, especially they of the circumcision: Whose mouths must be stopped, who overthrow entire households, teaching things which they should not, for filthy profit's sake."

Titus 1:10-11 AKJV

"But there were false prophets also among the people, even as there shall be false teachers among you... through greed shall they exploit you with false words..."

2 Peter 2:1,3 AKJV

WHAT MANY CHURCH LEADERS SAY...

THEIR JUSTIFICATION TO IMPOSE THE TITHE ON GOD'S PEOPLE:

- Abraham tithe before the law -

True, but only once and from the spoils of the war (no money involved). Abraham was not instructed by God to tithe and it became part of the law in Leviticus 27:30.

- Honor God with the tithe -

Proverbs 3:9 says "Honor the LORD with thy substance, and with the firstfruits of all thine increase." Sounds great, but such instructions were not ordered by Jesus or Paul in the New Testament for the New Testament believer.

- Church, just read Malachi 3:8 to 3:11 -

Ok, read it in context, so start with the first chapter:

Questions...

Mal 1:1 Whom is God speaking to?

Mal 2:1 Whom is God speaking to?

Mal 3:6 Whom is God speaking to?

Answers...

Mal 1:1 To the children of Israel

Mal 2:1 To all the priests

Mal 3:6 To the sons of Jacob

- God doesn't change -

True, His character never changes, God is Holy, Just, Righteous etc. Has nothing to do with the tithe!

- God's word doesn't change -

True, because He's preserved them through the King James Bible, and now through Arkman's King James Holy Bible... still has nothing to do with the tithe!

- God does not change His mind -

False, it's recorded in the Old Testament, when God did change His mind, read...

"And the LORD repented of the evil which He thought to do unto His people."

Exodus 32:14 AKJV

"... and God repented of the evil, that He had said that He would do unto them: and He did not."

Jonah 3:10 AKJV

"... and the LORD repented Him of the evil which He had pronounced against them..."

Jeremiah 26:19 AKJV

"for the priesthood being changed, there is made of necessity a change also of the law."

Hebrews 7:12 AKJV

- In the Old Testament, the widow woman gave the last meal she had to Prophet Elijah and God blessed her -

True, this account is recorded in 1 Kings, chapter 17... but first of all, the widow woman gave the prophet the last portion of food and not money. Additionally, she gave all and not a tenth and still, this has absolutely nothing to do with the tithe but rather everything to do with her response to God's prophet.

*** <u>Note:</u>

Do you know any prophet alive today with that type of mantle and or anointing?

- Poor widow gave her last 2 mites -

Here Jesus is commending the poor widow because she "gave all she had" while rich people were giving out of their abundance! This account is found twice in the gospels of Mark 12:41-44 and Luke 21:1-4.

*** _Note:_

There's no record of God instructing her to do this or that He blessed her for doing so, although (I do believe God would have blessed her). In any case, this still has nothing to do with the tithe!

- The Story of Ananias and Sapphira -
(Acts 4 and 5)

They "robbed God" by keeping part of the money from the land they sold that they were supposed to throw at the apostles' feet, so God killed them. They were supposed to give all the money and not a tenth.

True, money was collected for the sole purpose of distributing unto every man according to their needs! It is not recorded in scripture, where money was collected, received and used to build the apostle's own churches or ministries. The story of Ananias and Sapphira has nothing to do with the tithe!

4:34 ...for as many as were possessors of lands or houses sold them, and brought the money received...

4:35 And laid them down at the apostles' feet: and <u>distribution</u> was made unto every man according as he had need.

5:1 ...Ananias, with Sapphira his wife, sold land.

5:2 ...kept back part of the money... and brought only a part of it and laid it at the apostles' feet.

5:3 But Peter said, Ananias, why has Satan filled thine heart to lie to the Holy Ghost, and to keep back part of the money of the land?

5:5 And Ananias... fell down, and gave up the ghost...

5:10 Then fell she down immediately at his feet, and yielded up the ghost.

Acts 4:34,35; 5:1,2,3,5,10 AKJV

- Give out of your need; God will bless you because you cannot out give God -

God certainly knows that you can't give what you don't have! The Bible does not teach or instruct the New Testament believer to give out of their need and still, this has nothing to do with the tithe!

- Tithe! If you want to be blessed -

False, because your blessing and mine are tied-in directly on the strength of what Jesus did on Calvary... which was shedding His precious blood on the cross!!!

- Give and it shall be given unto you -

This scripture specifically refers to "mercy" (v36), not money and has nothing to do with the tithe!

"Be ye therefore merciful, as your Father also is merciful. Judge not, and ye shall not be judged: condemn not, and ye shall not be condemned: forgive, and ye shall be forgiven: Give, and it shall be given unto you; good measure, pressed down, and shaken together, and running over, shall men give into your bosom. For with the same measure that ye use as well it shall be measured to you again."

Luke 6:36-38 AKJV

- Don't tithe and God will curse you -

False, not according to the book of Galatians in the
New Testament:

*"... for it is written, (quoting from Deut. 27:26), Cursed
is everyone that continues not in all things which are
written in the book of the law to do them. Christ has
redeemed us from the curse of the law, being made a
curse for us..."*

Galatians 3:10 & 13 AKJV

*** <u>Note:</u>

My Jesus became a curse so that I would not be
cursed!!!

- Sow sparingly, and reap sparingly -

Paul is instructing the New Testament born again believer on how to give! Both of these verses have nothing to do with the tithe but everything to do with giving!

"But this I say, He which sows sparingly shall reap also sparingly; and he which sows bountifully shall reap also bountifully. Every man according as he purposes in his heart, so let him give; not grudgingly, or of necessity: for God loves a cheerful giver."

2 Corinthians 9:6-7 AKJV

- Church, I did not write the book; I'm not the author. The tithe is not my idea, but rather God's idea, so don't blame this thing on me -

You lying demon... you fully well know that tithing was God's ordinance strictly under the Old Covenant Law and it is not supposed to be enforced or imposed on God's people living under the dispensation of grace to all New Testament born again believers!!!

- Without the tithe in effect... How do the salaries and daily operations of a church get funded? -

1st - Where is your faith in God?
2nd - Church leaders are called to feed the poor, not to build their churches or their ministries!
Jesus clearly said... "I will build My church..."

Matthew 16:18 AKJV

"But my God shall supply all your needs according to His riches in glory by Christ Jesus."

Philippians 4:19 AKJV

- Does the Bible instruct the New Testament Believer "NOT" to tithe? -

No, because tithing was never an issue since the birth of the New Testament Church. No one tithe after Jesus resurrected, this is the reason why there are no records of any of the apostles or anyone else paying, giving, collecting or receiving the tithe from the books of Acts to Revelations. The instruction: Don't Tithe; was not necessary or needed to be part of the scriptures during the times when the apostles were writing the letters that addressed the early church.

Knowledge vs. Understanding

Part of the problem is that knowledge and understanding are not always the same and often it appears that these two are at war with each other!

Sadly, the body of Christ (especially church leaders) have the staggering ability to recite and quote the scriptures (knowledge), yet many lack the true understanding... of what they read!

The Pharisees and religious leaders during the time of Jesus were the most perfect examples of people having knowledge of God's word yet void of its understanding. Today, you don't have to look too far!

"Study to show thyself approved unto God, a workman that needs not to be ashamed, rightly dividing the word of truth!"

2 Timothy 2:15 AKJV

*"Then opened **Jesus** their understanding, that they might understand the scriptures,"*

Luke 24:45 AKJV

New Testament Confirmations:

OLD TESTAMENT:	VS.	NEW TESTAMENT:

... *God is one Lord*

Deut 6:4; Isa 46:9

... *God is one Lord*

Mk 12:29; 1 Cor 8:6

Love thy God...

Deut 6:5; 30:6

Love thy God...

Mt 22:37; Mk 12:30

Love thy neighbor...

Lev 19:18

Love thy neighbor...

Mt 5:43; Mk 12:31

The Tithe

Gen 14:20; Lev 27:30

Mal 3:8-10

NOT FOUND

no scriptures found!

UNCONFIRMED

*** <u>Note:</u>

The above comparisons show some of the most important commandments in the Old Testament that mostly Jesus and Paul confirmed in the New Testament. Notice that the tithe remains unconfirmed for the New Testament because there are no scriptures found that support the tithe for the New Testament born again believer.

The Old Testament ordinance and law of paying tithes were fulfilled when Jesus died and shed His precious blood on the cross!

"Think not that I Am come to destroy the law, or the prophets: I Am not come to destroy, but to fulfill."

Matthew 5:17 AKJV

More Warnings...

"Many will say to Me in that day, Lord, Lord, have we not prophesied in Thy name? and in Thy name have cast out devils? And in Thy name done many wonderful works? And then will I profess unto them, I never knew you: depart from Me, ye that work iniquity."

Matthew 7:22-23 AKJV

"... If any man shall add unto these things, God shall add unto him the plagues that are written in this book..."

Revelation 22:18-19 AKJV

"... for every man's word shall be his burden; for ye have perverted the words of the living God, of the LORD of Hosts our God."

Jeremiah 23:36 AKJV

This Is Thus Saith The LORD!!!

These (5) prophetic words spoken to me by the Holy Ghost specifically to be incorporated into this book as a prophetic warning and judgment to church leaders that choose to impose the tithe on God's people.

#1

"Tithing impoverishes My people and the driving force that enriches church leaders"

#2

"Will a man rob God? Yes, when church leaders impose the tithe on My people, church leaders are robbing Me by robbing My people"

#3

"As Pharaoh imposed his will on My people Israel, likewise church leaders impose the tithe on My people, the church"

#4

"And it came to pass in the course of time... Israel sighed by reason of their slavery, and they cried, and their cry came up unto God by reason of their slavery. And God heard their groaning, and God remembered His covenant with Abraham, with Isaac, and with Jacob. And God looked upon the children of Israel, and God had respect unto them."

Exodus 2:23-25 AKJV

"And the LORD said, I have surely seen the affliction of My people which are in Egypt, and have heard their cry by reason of their taskmasters; for I know their sorrows; and I Am come down to deliver them out of the hand of the Egyptians... Now therefore, behold, the

cry of the children of Israel is come unto Me: and I have also seen the oppression with which the Egyptians oppress them. Come now therefore, and I will send thee (**me**) unto Pharaoh (**church leaders**), that thou (**me**) may bring forth My people the children of Israel out of Egypt. And Moses said unto God, Who am I, that I should go unto Pharaoh, and that I should bring forth the children of Israel out of Egypt? And He said, Certainly I will be with thee (**me**)..."

Exodus 3:7-12 AKJV

#5

"God wants to set His church free from the curse and bondage of the tithe by delivering understanding, clarity and correction to the church leaders"

Prophetic warnings breakdown/significance:

These (5) prophetic words from the Holy Spirit were given to me within a two month span as I completed the work originally on my PowerPoint presentation that the LORD had commissioned me to put together. I would take and handle these prophetic words seriously because God most certainly is addressing the church leaders and He is issuing His warnings...

In prophetic word #1, the Holy Spirit is declaring His judgment on church leaders who continue to impose the tithe on God's people. First, God makes it very clear by making a distinction between <u>His</u> people and church leaders. He's not saying or using the word, <u>His</u> when addressing the church leaders! Second, God is also making very clear that the tithe is impoverishing His *people. The supernatural blessings the tithe commanded in the Old Testament are voided and nullified in the New Testament because this ordinance is not in effect for today or for the last 2,000 years! So the thing (tithing) that was a blessing in the Old Testament has become a curse in the New Testament!*

Part of this curse, is the driving force that continues to financially enrich church leaders all over this planet. I don't think God minds or cares that a church leader prospers, but He certainly cares about the venue the church leaders embrace and choose to prosper with!

In prophetic word #2, *the Holy Spirit is declaring exactly how He is being robbed. Although 95% of Christians would believe that people are robbing Him* by not paying "their tithes"... but they have it backwards! As far as God is concerned, He is being robbed every time a church leader imposes the tithe on God's people, by taking their money unlawfully by not following biblical pattern that was set in the book of 2 Corinthians 9:7 AKJV. In this scripture, the apostle Paul sets the guidelines for giving for every New Testament believer to follow. See the scripture below...

"Every man according as _he purposes in his heart_, so _let him give; not grudgingly, or of necessity_: for _God loves a cheerful giver_."

I believe the above scripture is the foundation for giving. Giving has replaced the tithe and God no longer commands His people to follow this Old Covenant law ordinance.

In prophetic word #3, the Holy Spirit is declaring clearly how He views and sees church leaders that impose the tithe on His people by comparing church leaders to pharaoh as mentioned in the book of Exodus. God also makes the comparison of the suffering and bondage of the children of Israel experienced to His Church today. You will see in Exodus, God warned pharaoh several times and then finally judged pharaoh and all his army by killing them all.

In prophetic word #4, the Holy Spirit is declaring the reason as for why He's warning church leaders that impose the tithe on God's people. The reason is that cry of the Church has come up to God's throne. God has finally heard the groanings of His people, and is getting ready to judge the church leaders but as a loving and merciful God, He is first warning the church leaders that have chosen their own ways to extract money from God's people by following the doctrines and ordinances of men rather than following the biblical pattern the LORD has instituted in the New Testament.

God sees His people as being afflicted by the curse of the tithe and has determined to set His people free from the curse and bondage of the tithe. But before He judges the church leaders and sets His people free, He must first warn the church leaders...

For some unknown reason, it's crystal clear that God has chosen me, as a vessel and servant to warn all the church leaders that chose to impose the tithe on God's people. Just as in Exodus 3, God commissions Moses to bring forth His people out of Egypt; God has also commissioned me to bring forth His people out from the *curse of the tithe! Besides commissioning me, the Holy Spirit also declares that He will be with me as He was with Moses!!!*

In prophetic word #5, the Holy Spirit is declaring His divine purpose which is to set His church free from the curse and bondage caused by the tithe by delivering understanding, clarity and correction to the church leaders who impose the tithe on God's people!

Conclusion:

The purpose of this book is very clear... God is issuing a warning to church leaders that impose the tithe on God's people. God wants to set His people free from the curse and bondage of the tithe. God has provided clarity and understanding through this book to accomplish all that He has purposed!

The act or action of imposing the tithe on God's people is something that has been taught and handed down to many church leaders for the last few generations. If you've never heard about the tithe, and one day you decide that you want to read the entire Bible, you will surely conclude (after reading the Bible), that the tithe was to be observed only by the Hebrews in the Old Testament under the ordinance and requirement of the Old Covenant.

I have met countless of precious brothers and sisters and New Testament believers, who have confided and told me that they still live under condemnation, guilt and fear (that God is going to curse them) because (not having food to put on their table to feed their children and not having enough money to pay their rent when due) has caused them to missed paying the tithes (as required by their church) in the past (weeks at a time) and because living in fear, that God will surely curse them now... they have become some of the most miserable people living on the face of this earth. Under those ungodly conditions... please ask yourself and tell me, why someone would want to be a Christian?

My advice to the Church is... judge the words that come out from the pulpit, radio or TV by researching and studying the Holy Scriptures. Also, if you ever disagree with anything said from the pulpit... you have the right to approach your church leader (privately) and inquire about how and why you disagree with him or her.

Many church leaders (when it comes to giving) lack the understanding of the scriptures... this is one of the reasons why, they impose the tithe on God's people because their lack of understanding motivates them to follow after the doctrines and commandments of men. This continues to be the ongoing sad state and condition of the Church today. It is not surprising, that we do not see the miracles (in the Church today) in the dimension that was witnessed from the book of Acts.

Giving cheerfully has replaced the tithe. The tithe should never be imposed/enforced on the body of Christ ever! Remember that throughout the New Testament (from Acts to Revelation), every time any of the apostles collected money from the Church, it was specifically used to feed the poor... no record exists in the New Testament of money ever being collected by the apostles for the specific use to support the Church, the ongoing day by day operations or church leaders' salaries.

My advice to the church leaders... Heed to what the Holy Spirit is saying because... You have been WARNED!!!

Scripture references taken from:

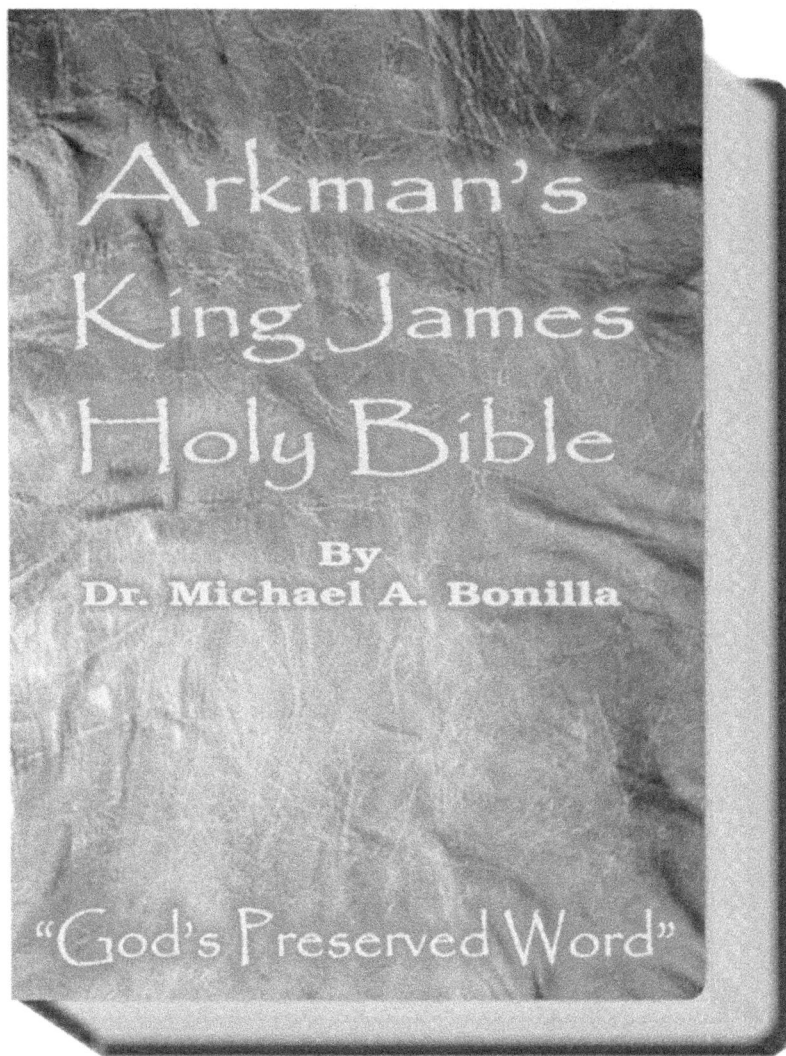

Available (free) at <u>www.akjv.org</u>

Available presentations/seminars

in PowerPoint:

1). The 5 Major Discoveries: Noah's Ark; Sodom and Gomorrah: The Exodus Route, The Red Crossing Site and Mount Sinai; The Crucifixion Site of Jesus, the Ark of the Covenant and the Blood of Jesus.

2). Creation, Dinosaurs and Noah's Ark.

3). Dinosaurs and the Bible.

4). The Dangers of Evolution.

5). Bible Version Wars™ (restricted).

6). King James vs. Reina Valera (restricted).

7). THE TITHE: Blessing or Curse?

To schedule a seminar/presentations

for your church, group or college, please contact me at:

Bonilla Archaeological Research

www.arkman.net

Office #: (631) 745-2269

Bonus materials:

Noah's Ark
(Nuhun Gemisi)
Ararat, Turkey
18½ miles south of Mt. Ararat

Genesis 6:15

300 x 50 x 30 cubits = 515'L x 85'9"W x 51'5"H

Note: Royal Egyptian Cubit = 20.62"

Location:	Latitude:	Longitude:	Elevation:
A Noah's Ark	39°26'26.0" N	44°14'05.0" E	6,525'
— Mt. Ararat	39°42'07.0" N	44°17'49.0" E	16,946'

Bonilla Archaeological Research™
www.arkman.net
Recorded/Documented on 10/11/00 by Dr. Michael A. Bonilla

64

The Tomb of Jesus

The Borrowed Tomb of Jesus, the way it looks today!

"Now in the place where He was crucified there was a garden; and in the garden a new sepulchre, wherein was never man yet laid." John 19:41 AKJV

... the way it looked almost 2,000 years ago!

BONILLA ARCHAEOLOGICAL RESEARCH™ 2014©

The Crucifixion Site Scene of Jesus

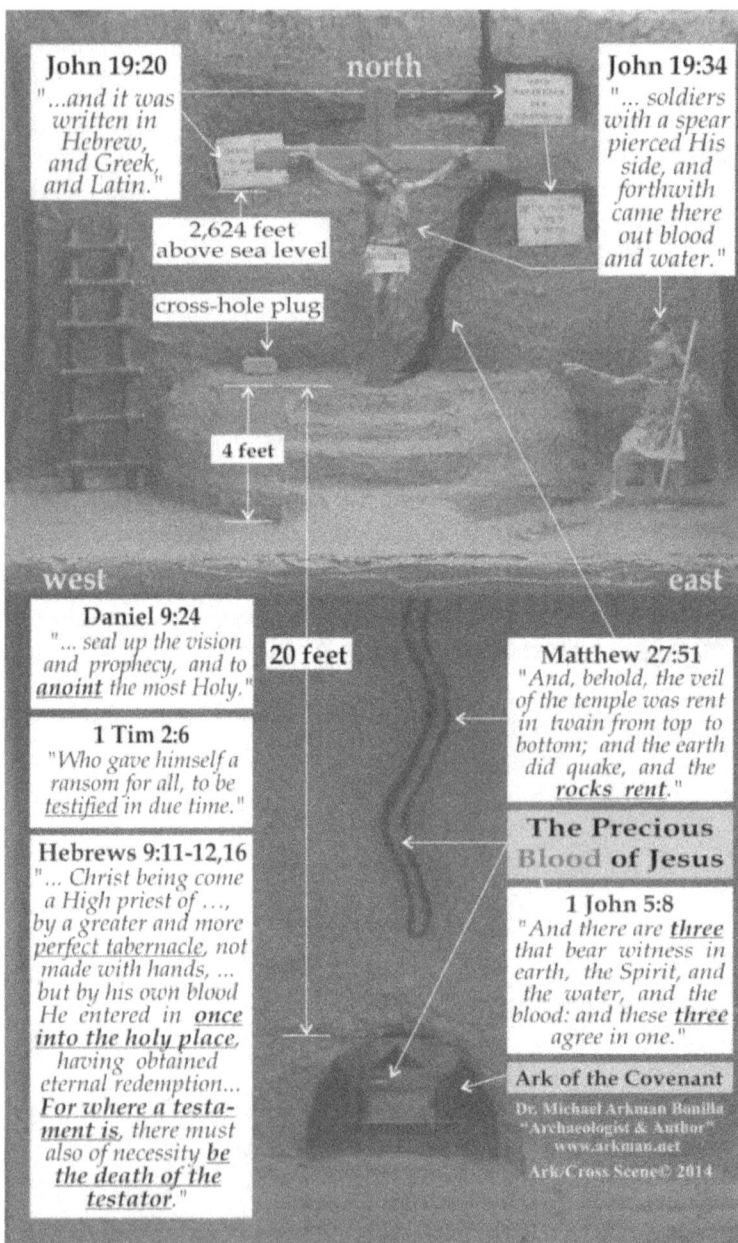

John 19:20
"...and it was written in Hebrew, and Greek, and Latin."

north

John 19:34
"... soldiers with a spear pierced His side, and forthwith came there out blood and water."

2,624 feet above sea level

cross-hole plug

4 feet

west

east

Daniel 9:24
"... seal up the vision and prophecy, and to **anoint** the most Holy."

20 feet

1 Tim 2:6
"Who gave himself a ransom for all, to be **testified** in due time."

Hebrews 9:11-12,16
"... Christ being come a High priest of ..., by a greater and more **perfect tabernacle**, not made with hands, ... but by his own blood He entered in **once into the holy place**, having obtained eternal redemption... **For where a testament is**, there must also of necessity **be the death of the testator**."

Matthew 27:51
"And, behold, the veil of the temple was rent in twain from top to bottom; and the earth did quake, and the **rocks rent**."

The Precious Blood of Jesus

1 John 5:8
"And there are **three** that bear witness in earth, the Spirit, and the water, and the blood: and these **three** agree in one."

Ark of the Covenant

Dr. Michael Arkman Bonilla
"Archaeologist & Author"
www.arkman.net
Ark/Cross Scene© 2014

66

www.ingramcontent.com/pod-product-compliance
Lightning Source LLC
Chambersburg PA
CBHW021212020426

42331CB00003B/323